She Plays Sports

She Plays Volleyball

By Trudy Becker

level 2 little blue readers

www.littlebluehousebooks.com

Little Blue House is distributed by North Star Editions:
sales@northstareditions.com | 888-417-0195

Produced for Little Blue House by Red Line Editorial.

Photographs ©: Shutterstock Images, cover (background), 4, 11, 24 (bottom right); iStockphoto, cover (girl), 7, 9, 12, 15, 16, 19, 21, 23, 24 (top left), 24 (top right), 24 (bottom left)

Library of Congress Control Number: 2022910481

ISBN
978-1-64619-712-5 (hardcover)
978-1-64619-744-6 (paperback)
978-1-64619-804-7 (ebook pdf)
978-1-64619-776-7 (hosted ebook)

Printed in the United States of America
Mankato, MN
012023

About the Author

Trudy Becker lives in Minneapolis, Minnesota. She likes exploring new places and loves anything involving books.

Table of Contents

Getting Ready

I play volleyball.

I love match days.

I get ready to play.

I need many things
for matches.
I always wear my uniform.
I look like my teammates,
and I can move easily.

uniform

I put on my
volleyball shoes.
The shoes grip the court
so I will not slip.
I wear kneepads to
protect myself too.

kneepad

I grab my water bottle.
When I am thirsty, I can take a drink.
I put everything in my bag.

water bottle

net

On the Court

On match days, I go to the volleyball court.

The court has a long net in the middle.

One team stays on each side.

My coach talks to
the team.
We always focus and
play hard.
We want to win
every match.

coach

In the Match

I run onto the court before each match starts. Both teams stand in their positions. One player tosses the ball into the air and hits it.

When the ball flies to my team's side, I can't let it touch the floor.

I put out my arms.

I bump the ball.

bump

Sometimes I play close to the net.
When the ball flies over, I can jump up and block it.

My team works together.
Sometimes teammates
hit the ball to me.
I jump and spike it.
I score!
I love volleyball.

spike

Glossary

bump

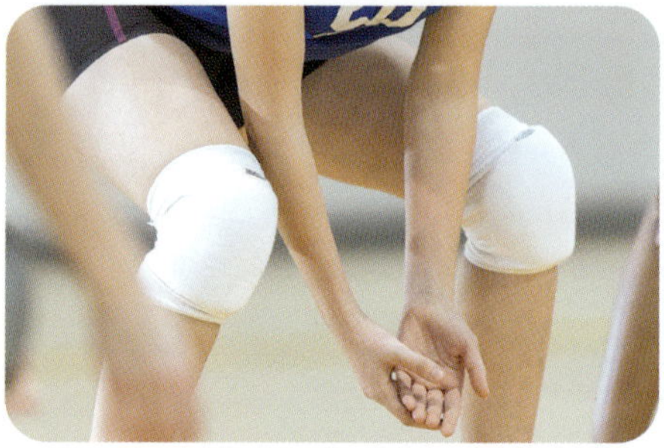

kneepads

court

net

Index